The Widow's Resource

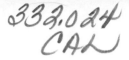

The Widow's Resource

How to Solve the Financial and Legal
Problems That Occur Within the First Six
to Nine Months of Your Husband's Death

Julie A. Calligaro

Women's Source Books Publishers
Grosse Ile, Michigan

THE WIDOW'S RESOURCE
How to Solve the Financial and Legal Problems That Occur Within the
First Six to Nine Months of Your Husband's Death

Julie A. Calligaro

Women's Source Books Publishers,
Post Office Box 99
Grosse Ile, Michigan 48138 U.S.A.

Library of Congress Catalog Card Number 96-61700

Printed in the United States of America
Book design Sans Serif
Cover design Allessandra White, Goetzcraft Printers, Inc.

Cataloging in Publication Data:

    Calligaro, Julie A.
    The widow's resource: how to solve the financial and legal prob-
lems that occur within the first six to nine months of your husband's
death / Julie A. Calligaro.
    p. cm.
    Includes index.
    Preassigned LCCN: 96-61799
    ISBN: 1-890117-03-X

    1. Widows—United States—Life skills guides. 2. Widowhood—
United States. I. Title.

HQ1058.5.U5C35 1997   305.48'9654
                QBI96-2568

CONTENTS

CONTENTS

NOTE

This book is intended as a resource. It is sold with the understanding that the publisher and author are not engaged in rendering legal, accounting or financial services. If legal, accounting or financial services are required, seek a professional advisor.

Although every precaution has been taken in the preparation of this book, the publisher and author assume no responsibility for errors or omissions.Neither is any liability assumed for damages resulting from the use of information contained in this book.

The publisher and author specifically disclaim any liability, loss or risk, personal or otherwise which is incurred as a direct or indirect consequence of the use and application of the contents of this book.

ACKNOWLEDGMENT

I gratefully acknowledge the invaluable contributions of Julia M. Demery, Bonnie L. Miller, Clinton Meyering and Nicholas P. Scavone. Thank you.

HOW TO USE THIS BOOK

This book will help you solve the financial and legal problems that occur within the first six to nine months of your husband's death.

I realize that you feel your life is out of control. You are depressed and angry. You have difficulty making decisions. Your energy level is low. You are on an emotional roller coaster, crying one minute and laughing the next.

What you are experiencing is natural and, more importantly, it is temporary. You will regain control. Your depression and the anger will abate. Your ability to make decisions will return. Your energy level will return to normal. And your emotions will stabilize.

Unfortunately the financial and legal issues that occur immediately after your husband's death will not wait until you are feeling like yourself again. These problems cannot be ignored or put on a back burner until you feel ready to tackle them.

And that is exactly why I have written this book. "The Widow's Resource" will guide you through the financial and legal problems that will occur immediately after your husband's death.

Each chapter discusses a specific financial or legal topic. Read each chapter, even the ones that don't seem to apply to you. Otherwise you may overlook something that is relevant to your situation.

Each chapter includes a "To Do List" that specifies the actions that you should take to resolve the problems discussed in the chapter. The To Do Lists are repeated on perforated pages at the end of the book. After reading a chapter, tear out the chapter's To Do List from the perforated pages and work through the list.

The sooner you begin, the sooner you will have these problems under control. You will also feel a sense of accomplishment as you complete (and cross off) the actions listed on the To Do Lists.

You have the ability to solve these problems without my help, but following the suggestions contained in this book will ease you through this period of uncertainty and transition. Don't procrastinate, turn to Chapter 1 and begin. Good Luck!

I welcome your comments and questions, and I would appreciate hearing how this book helped you and how it could have been more helpful. Please write to Julie A. Calligaro at P.O. Box 99, Grosse Ile, MI 48138.

1

As You Begin

Preparing to function efficiently and effectively

Your objective as you work through Chapter 1 is to prepare yourself and your surroundings so that you function efficiently and effectively.

ESTABLISH A WORKSPACE

Establish a permanent workspace by setting aside a table or desk for correspondence and recordkeeping. If you have a personal computer and are comfortable using it, organize your workspace around your computer.

At an office supply store buy a box of legal size manila folders, a pocket or wall calendar, several legal pads, an inexpensive and easy to use calculator, a box of plain stationery with envelopes, and a 12" by 18" plastic storage box with cover. At the post office buy a roll of stamps.

MAINTAIN YOUR PHYSICAL AND EMOTIONAL HEALTH

If you are physically and emotionally healthy you will have strength and energy to meet the challenges ahead.

Physical Health

There are several simple steps you can take to improve or maintain your physical health.

Eat healthy foods in sensible quantities. You may not have the energy to plan meals, buy groceries and prepare food; you should, however, have nourishing yet easy-to-prepare foods readily available. For example, stock your freezer with oven-or microwave-ready meals that appeal to you or make a large pot of soup which will last several days. In addition, meet a friend or co-worker for lunch or dinner regularly.

If you were physically active before your husband's death, resume the physical activity immediately. If you don't have the energy for your former workout, use walking as an interim exercise. Whenever possible walk with a friend, neighbor or co-worker and you will be able to exercise and have someone to talk to at the same time.

If you were not physically active before your husband's death, begin a modest program of physical activity today. For instance, buy a pair of comfortable walking shoes and take short walks every day (rain or shine).

As you build stamina, increase the distance you

walk. If you have friends, co-workers or neighbors who walk regularly, join them.

Emotional Health

Depression, sadness, loneliness and feelings of guilt because, at times, you are happy are all a part of the grieving process.

If you feel you would benefit from professional counseling, seek out a competent and caring professional. Ask your friends, family, co-workers, doctor or minister for recommendations.

If you are not interested in professional counseling, consider joining one of the many support groups whose members have also lost their spouses. Your church or community may sponsor such a group.

If you cannot find a suitable support group, seek out other women who have lost their spouses. It will help you to talk to others who have had similar feelings.

The comfort and companionship of others will help you fill the enormous void created by your husband's death. Spend time with people who are sensitive to you and are good listeners.

Make plans to do something with another person at least weekly and at holidays, birthdays and the anniversaries of your wedding and your spouse's death.

Reach out to your family and your friends for support and be receptive when they reach out to you.

Spiritual Self

Many women relate that their faith in God sustained and supported them through their grief. Don't overlook your spiritual needs or your spiritual resources.

A Feeling of Security

If you are living alone there are several simple and inexpensive things you can do to maintain a feeling of security.

Give a spare house or apartment key to a trusted family member or friend.

Conceal a spare key outside your home and tell a trusted family member or friend where the key is located. Use your ingenuity but don't be too clever; a key that your family or friend can't find defeats the purpose. Don't draw attention to yourself as you conceal the key.

Install timers on a TV or radio and on several conspicuous lights throughout your home. Set the timers to turn on the TV or radio and the lights when you will be away from home for an extended period of time and when you come into an empty house after dark.

Timers cost less than $20 and can be purchased at a hardware store or home improvement center. They are easy to install and set; if you can set an alarm clock you can set a timer.

Place a spare car key in a magnetic key box and attach the box to a concealed but accessible spot on the outside of your car. Again, don't attract attention to yourself as you conceal the key box. Magnetic key boxes cost less than $2 and can be purchased at a car wash.

Consider a pet, not just for security but for companionship as well.

TO DO LIST

Establish Your Workspace:

"Shopping List":

❑ a box of legal size manila folders

❑ pocket or wall calendar

❑ several legal pads

❑ cheap, easy to use calculator

❑ plain stationery and envelopes

❑ 12" by 18" storage box with cover

❑ roll of stamps

To Do:

❑ Set aside a permanent workspace with desk or table.

" Physical Health"

❑ Eat healthy foods in sensible quantities.

❑ Stock easy to prepare, nourishing and appealing foods.

❑ Meet a friend for lunch or dinner regularly.

❑ Resume former physical activity or,

❑ Buy a pair of comfortable walking shoes, and

❑ Take short walks daily, increasing the distance as you build stamina.

"Emotional Health"

❑ Consider professional counseling.

❑ Ask family or friends for recommendations.

❑ Make an appointment with the counselor.

❑ Locate a support group whose members have lost their spouses.

❑ Learn the date, time and location of the next meeting.

❑ Contact a member and ask them to accompany you to the next meeting.

❑ Go to the meeting.

❑ Seek out other women who have lost their spouses.

❑ Speak to a family member or friend by phone every day.

❑ Make plans for holidays, birthdays and anniversaries.

"Spiritual Self"

❑ Draw from your spiritual resources.

❑ Satisfy your spiritual needs.

A Feeling Of Security

"Shopping List":

❑ extra house keys and an extra car key

❑ magnetic box for car key

❑ timers

To Do:

❑ Give a spare house key to trusted family member or friend.

❑ Conceal a spare house key outside and tell a trusted family member or friend of the location.

❑ Install the timers on TV or radio and conspicuous lights.

❑ Set the timers to turn on the TV or radio and lights when you will be away for an extended period and anytime you come into an empty house after dark.

❑ Conceal a spare car key in a magnetic key box in an accessible place on your car.

2

GETTING ORGANIZED

Locating and organizing essential information

Your objective as you work through Chapter 2 is to locate and organize essential information.

RECORDKEEPING

If your husband was the family "record-keeper" before his death, that responsibility will now be yours. Take the time to set up an efficient recordkeeping system and eliminate the frustration that comes from searching for something that you know you have but just can't find. File all important papers in separate manila folders. Label each folder and place them in alphabetical order in a large storage box.

INFORMATION TO LOCATE AND ORGANIZE

During the next few months you will need specific items of information. If you take the time to locate and organize the information now you will save time and energy later on.

The information you will need to locate and organize is:

1. Identification numbers,
2. Specific documents,
3. Information that may be located in a Safe Deposit Box,
4. Information about tax, legal and financial advisors,
5. A reminder system, and
6. An inventory of your assets and debts.

IDENTIFICATION NUMBERS

What identification numbers will I need?

Label a manila folder "Identification Numbers." On a sheet of paper list your husband's date of birth, social security number, and military service number; your social security number and your children's social security numbers if they are minors. Insert the list into the folder and place the folder in the storage box.

DOCUMENTS

What documents will I need?

Locate the following documents:

1. Tax returns for the last three years.
2. Your husband's will, if one exists.
3. Your husband's military discharge papers, if he was in the military.
4. Any insurance policies insuring your husband's life.
5. Fifteen certified copies of your husband's death certificate.
6. Birth certificates for all family members.
7. Marriage license.
8. Closing or escrow papers you received when you purchased real estate.
9. A "Buy-Sell Agreement" and all other documents related to your husband's ownership of a business.
10. Divorce judgment or decree if you were divorced from a former husband.

As you locate an item, place it in a separate manila folder, label the folder, and store the folder in alphabetical order in the storage box.

SAFE DEPOSIT BOX

What do I do if there is a safe deposit box?

If you have a safe deposit box label a folder "Safe Deposit Box." Go to the bank where the box is located, taking with you the key to the box, a note pad, pen or pencil and a brief case or bag that closes securely.

Retrieve the box and take it to a private room. If the following items are in the box remove them:

1. Husband's will.
2. Insurance policies.
3. Husband's military discharge papers.
4. Birth certificates.
5. Marriage license.
6. Real estate documents.
7. The Buy-Sell Agreement and all other documents related to your husband's ownership of a business.

Make a complete list of the items that you return to the box. When you return home, label folders for the items you removed from the box. Store the folders in alphabetical order in the storage box. In the "Safe Deposit Box" folder insert the list of the items you left in the safe deposit box.

ADVISORS

Do I need to contact an accountant, attorney or financial advisor?

During the next few months you may need to consult one or more of these professional advisors. Take the time to select an accountant, attorney, and financial advisor.

At this point you will only be choosing the advisors that you may need to consult in the future. Later chapters will discuss when you should actually contact the advisor.

Tax advisor

Label a manila folder "Advisors." Inside the folder list the name, address and phone number of the accountant who prepared last year's tax returns. You will need professional tax advice if you will be receiving survivor's benefits from your husband's pension or if an estate tax return must be filed. If you and your husband did not consult an accountant in the past, ask family members or friends for recommendations. List the name, address and phone number of the recommended individuals in the "Advisors" folder.

Legal advisor

List the name, address, and phone number of the attorney who represented you and your husband in the past. If you have not been represented by an attorney, or if you are not comfortable with the attorney who represented you, ask family and friends for recommendations and list the name, address and phone number in your "Advisors" folder. In Chapter 8 you will evaluate if it's necessary to probate your husband's estate. If a probate is necessary, you will need to consult an attorney.

Financial advisor

If you and your husband worked with a financial advisor or stock broker, list the name, address and phone number in your "Advisors" folder.

REMINDER CALENDAR

How do I keep track of deadlines and important dates?

A Reminder Calendar alerts you to deadlines and important dates and helps you keep track of checks and other items that you are expecting to receive by mail.

How do I set up a Reminder Calendar?

Locate the calendar you purchased at the office supply. A pocket calendar may be easier to work with than a wall calendar but use whatever is readily available.

Write a brief description of each deadline directly on the calendar at the date at which the deadline occurs. Also write on the calendar, a reasonable number of days **BEFORE** the date of the deadline, a reminder of the deadline and the date of the deadline.

For example, your federal and state tax returns will be due April 15th. On the calendar at April 15, write "Tax returns due today". Also record a reminder to yourself a reasonable number of days before the date of the deadline so that you have sufficient time to complete the task. In this example you would write on the calendar space at March 15, "Tax returns due April 15th."

Also use your Reminder Calendar to keep track of items that you are expecting to receive by mail. For example, if your husband's employer said you will receive an application for benefits by May 7th, write on the calendar space at May 7 "Form received from XYZ Employer?"

A Reminder Calendar is an invaluable tool. It forces you to keep track of important dates and it frees you from the responsibility of having to remember so many things at once. To be useful, however, you must enter every important deadline on the Reminder Calendar **AND** you must review the calendar **EVERY SINGLE DAY**. Place the calendar in a location that allows you to use it regularly and review it daily.

INVENTORY OF ASSETS AND DEBTS (LIABILITIES)

Why should I take inventory of my assets and debts?

An inventory will tell you the amount of your assets and the amount of your debts. It will list your current debts so that you don't neglect any payments. And it will enable you to determine if you need to probate your husband's estate.

How do I take inventory of my assets and debts?

1. Gather information about each of your assets and each of your debts (liabilities). For example, bank statements, statements of brokerage accounts and mutual funds, stock certificates, savings bonds, tax bills or appraisals to determine the value of real estate, statements of mortgage balances, loan balances and credit card balances.

2. Insert the information in separate folders and label the folders. Avoid the temptation to file all the information in one or two folders.

3. Tear out the Inventory from the perforated section at the end of the book. Consulting the information you have accumulated in the folders, record the value of each asset and the amount of each debt.

4. Also indicate on the Inventory how each asset is titled. The assets will be titled either in your husband's name, your name, both names (joint ownership) or in the name of a trust.

5. Place the folders in alphabetical order in the storage box.

You may not be able to complete certain sections of the Inventory until you read later chapters of the book. For example, you may not know the amount of life insurance proceeds (Chapter 3); or the amount of retirement benefits (Chapter 5).

Where will I find the information that I will need to complete the Inventory?

a. Safe deposit box.
b. Fireproof box or safe in your home.
c. Desk or file cabinet.
d. Your husband's desk or file cabinet at work.
e. Computer files.

Should I be concerned if I don't have all of the assets and debts listed on the Inventory?

No. The Inventory is a comprehensive list of the assets commonly accumulated and the debts commonly incurred during marriage. Expect to see assets and debts on the Inventory that do not apply to you.

Should I be selling assets at this time?

Your ability to make reasonable decisions may be temporarily impaired. I recommend that you defer all non-essential decisions for six to nine months. By then you will be ready and able to make sensible decisions based on your circumstances and your objectives.

Therefore, unless you are facing a financial emergency, postpone making decisions about the following assets:

1. Whether or not to sell your home,
2. Whether or not to sell your husband's business,
3. Whether or not to sell other assets (i.e., other real estate, stocks, bonds),
4. How to invest your life insurance proceeds.

INVENTORY

ASSETS

Type of Asset   **Current Value of Asset**

How Asset is Titled (H = Husband, W = Wife,
                   J = Joint, T = Asset in a Trust)

Asset	Value	Title
I. Cash Assets		
1. Cash on hand	_____	_____
2. Life Insurance (See Chapter 3)	_____	_____
3. Checking Account(s) (Bank and Credit Union)		
	_____	_____
	_____	_____
	_____	_____
4. Savings Account(s) (Bank and Credit Union)		
	_____	_____
	_____	_____
	_____	_____

5. Money Market Account(s) _____ _____

    _____ _____

   Total Cash Assets _____

II. Investment Assets

1. Certificate(s) of Deposit _____ _____

    _____ _____

2. Treasury Bills _____ _____

3. Stocks (List the company, number of shares and the current price per share)

Company	Shares	Price Per Share	Total
_____	_____	_____	_____
_____	_____	_____	_____
_____	_____	_____	_____
_____	_____	_____	_____

   Total Stocks _____

4. Mutual Funds (List the fund, number of shares and the price per share)

Company	Shares	Price Per Share	Total
_____	_____	_____	_____
_____	_____	_____	_____
_____	_____	_____	_____
_____	_____	_____	_____

    Total Mutual Funds _____

5. U.S. Savings Bonds _____
6. Municipal Bonds _____
7. Corporate Bonds _____

    Total Investment Assets _____

III. Real Estate

1. Residence _____
2. Vacation Home _____
3. Vacant Land _____

    Total Real Estate Assets _____

IV. Retirement/Pension/Profit Sharing

1. IRA Accounts (Include lump sum distributions rolled over from your husband's pension plan, Chapter 5)   _____

2. Keogh Accounts   _____

3. Pension/Profit Sharing Plans (401K, Thrift Savings, Stock Purchase)   _____

   Total Retirement/Pension/ Profit Sharing   _____

V. Miscellaneous

1. Limited Partnerships   _____

2. Notes, Mortgages or Other Debts Owed To You   _____

3. Other   _____

        _____

   Total Miscellaneous Assets   _____

21

VI. Business Ownership (See Chap.9) _____

TOTALS OF ASSETS:

I.   Cash _____

II. Investment Assets _____

III. Real Estate Assets _____

IV. Retirement Assets _____

V. Miscellaneous Assets _____

VI. Business Ownership Assets _____

TOTAL VALUE OF ALL ASSETS _____

DEBTS (LIABILITIES)

Type of Debt   **Outstanding Balance**

1. Mortgage (Residence) _____

2. Mortgage (Vacation Home) _____

3. Home Equity Loan _____

4. Auto Loan _____

5. Auto Loan _____

6. Credit Card _____

7. Credit Card _____

8. Credit Card _____

9. Life Insurance Loan   _____

10. Other Loan(s)   _____

   TOTAL DEBT   _____

Insert the Inventory in a folder labeled "Inventory." You will be adding information to the Inventory as you work through other chapters. After you read Chapter 6, calculate your Net Worth.

NET WORTH:

TOTAL OF ALL ASSETS   _____

MINUS TOTAL DEBT   _____

YOUR NET WORTH IS   _____

TO DO LIST

FROM THIS POINT FORWARD INSTRUCTIONS TO LABEL, ALPHABETIZE AND STORE A FOLDER OR FOLDERS WILL BE ABBREVIATED "LASF"

Identification Numbers

❑ Label a folder

❑ In the folder list husband's:

- social security number
- date of birth
- military service number

❑ List your social security number and your children's numbers if they are minors.

❑ LASF

Documents

Locate:

❑ Your husband's will. LASF

❑ Tax returns for the last three years. LASF

❑ All insurance policies. LASF

❑ Your husband's military discharge papers. LASF

❑ Fifteen certified copies of your husband's death certificate. LASF

❑ Birth certificates for all family members. LASF

❑ Your marriage license. LASF

❑ Closing or escrow papers received when you purchased real estate. LASF

❑ Your divorce judgment if previously divorced. LASF

❑ Buy-Sell Agreement and other documents related to your husband's business. LASF

Safe Deposit Box

❑ Label a folder "Safe Deposit Box".

❑ In the folder list the location and number of the box.

❑ Take the key, a note pad, pen or pencil and a briefcase or similar bag that closes securely to the bank and retrieve the box.

❑ Remove these items from the box:

- husband's will
- insurance policies
- military discharge papers
- birth certificates for family members
- marriage license

- real estate documents
- divorce judgment
- documents related to your husband's ownership of a business

❑ Make a written inventory of the contents remaining in the box.

❑ Label folders for the items you removed from the box.

❑ LASF.

Advisors

❑ Label a folder "Advisors".

❑ List name, address and phone number of:

- accountant
- attorney
- stockbroker or financial advisor

Reminder Calendar

❑ Record all deadlines on the date of the deadline and a reasonable number of days before the deadline.

❑ Record all items that you are to receive by a certain date on that date.

❑ **REVIEW YOUR REMINDER CALENDAR DAILY**.

Inventory of Assets and Debts

❑ Gather information about each asset and each debt in a separate folder.

❑ Record the value of each asset and the amount of each debt on the perforated Inventory.

❑ LASF for each asset and each debt.

3

APPLYING FOR
INSURANCE BENEFITS

Your objective in Chapter 3 is to determine if you are entitled to insurance benefits and, if so, to apply for them.

If you are entitled to insurance benefits, you will not receive the money until you file the necessary forms. And, most insurance companies do not pay interest on the money. So, the sooner you get the ball rolling by applying for the benefits, the sooner you will receive the insurance money and be able to put it to work for you.

LIFE INSURANCE

There are two types of life insurance policies to consider:

1. Policies provided by your husband's employer.
2. Policies purchased by you and your husband.

How do I find out if there is a policy provided by my husband's employer and, if so, apply for the benefits?

Whether your husband was employed or retired at his death he may be covered under a group life insurance policy provided by his employer.

Label a folder "Life Insurance-Employer." Inside the folder note the employer's name, address and phone number. Contact the department that administers employee benefits and ask if your husband is covered under a group life insurance policy.

If there is coverage, ask if you are the beneficiary. If you are the beneficiary, ask what the procedure is for applying for the benefits. Follow the procedure and apply for the benefits.

How do I apply for life insurance benefits for a policy or policies that my husband and I paid for?

Label a folder "Life Insurance-XYZ Company". Contact the insurance company by following the procedure described in the section entitled "How do I contact the insurance company?" and ask if you are the beneficiary. If you are the beneficiary, ask what the procedure is for applying for the benefits. Follow the procedure and apply for the benefits.

How do I contact the insurance company?
If you have an insurance agent:

If you have an insurance agent, add the agent's name, address and phone number to the company's "Life Insurance" folder. Contact the agent and tell him or her that you want to file a claim for life insurance benefits.

The insurance agent will send you the appropriate form and instructions for applying for the benefits. Follow the instructions and apply for the benefits.

If you do not have an insurance agent:

If you have located insurance policies but do not have an agent, look up the insurance company in the phone book or call information and ask for a local phone number. Call the company and ask for the necessary forms to file a claim for life insurance benefits.

If you cannot find a phone number, write to the company at the address listed on the policy. In your letter refer to the policy number (which you will find on the policy itself), tell the company you want to apply for life insurance benefits and ask for the appropriate claim form and instructions for applying for the benefits.

Sample Letter:

XYZ Insurance Company   Date
123 Boston Boulevard
Detroit, MI 48000

Re: (Your husband's name)
Policy 000000

Dear Claims Agent,
    I wish to apply for the life insurance benefits provided by the policy referenced above. Please send me the necessary forms and instructions for applying for the benefits.
    My address is:
    My phone number is:
                    Yours truly,

Make a copy of the letter before you mail it and place the copy in the appropriate manila folder. On your Reminder Calendar enter "Receipt of claim form" for 10 days after your phone call or letter to the insurance company. If you have not received the form by the 11th day, contact the company again.

What if I think there is a life insurance policy or policies that my husband and I paid for but I cannot find the policy?

If you have correspondence from an insurance company or canceled checks of payments made to an insurance company, there may be a life insurance policy in effect.

Send a letter to the company to determine if there is a life insurance policy.

Sample Letter:

XYZ Insurance Company   Date
123 Boston Boulevard
Detroit, MI 48000

Re: (Your husband's name)
Policy 000000

Dear Claims Agent,
    I have reason to believe that your company issued a life insurance policy insuring the life of _____. However I have not located the actual policy.
    Please confirm if a policy is in effect and, if so, the name of the beneficiary. If a policy is in effect and if I am the beneficiary, please send me the necessary form and instructions for applying for the benefits.
    My address is:
    My phone number is:
                        Yours truly,

Once I receive a claim form from the insurance company, how do I apply for the benefits?

1. Follow the directions on the claim form.

2. If you have questions call the person whose name appears on the letter that accompanied the claim form.
3. Write a cover letter.

Sample Letter:

XYZ Insurance Company   Date
123 Boston Boulevard
Detroit, MI 48000

Re: (Your husband's name)
Policy 000000

Dear Claims Agent,
   I enclose the completed claim form, a certified death certificate and the insurance policy. Please send the check to me at this address:
   My phone number is:
                            Thank you,

Make a copy of the your cover letter, the claim form, and the insurance policy and insert them in the appropriate manila folder. Mail the original claim form, a certified death certificate and the actual policy to the insurance company at the address specified in the instructions.

On your Reminder Calendar enter "Receipt of check from XYZ" for 10 days. If you have not received the check by the 11th day, call the company. Use your Reminder Calendar and be persistent.

What if I am not the beneficiary, should I still apply for the benefits?

If you are not the beneficiary there is no point in applying for the benefits **unless**:

- your minor child (children) is the beneficiary, or,
- the primary beneficiary is deceased and there is no living secondary beneficiary, or
- your husband's estate is the beneficiary.

In any of these circumstances, however, you will have to begin a Probate before you can apply for the benefits. (See Chapter 8).

Fraternal Organizations

Your husband may have purchased a life insurance policy from a fraternal organization, such as the Knights of Columbus. Regardless of who issued the policy, the procedure for applying for the benefits is the same:

1. locate the policy;
2. locate the insurance company;
3. determine who is the beneficiary;
4. if you are the beneficiary, determine the procedure for applying for benefits;
5. apply for the benefits.

Cancer Policies

A Cancer Policy pays a death benefit if the person whose life was insured dies of cancer. If your husband's death was caused by cancer and his life was insured by a cancer policy, file a claim for benefits. The procedure for applying for the benefits is the same:

1. locate the policy;
2. locate the insurance company;
3. determine who is the beneficiary;
4. if you are the beneficiary, determine the procedure for applying for benefits;
5. apply for the benefits.

Credit Unions

Some loans from credit unions include death benefits. If your husband had a loan or loans from a credit union, contact the loan department of the credit union and ask if the loan includes a death benefit. Be prepared with the loan number and your account number when you make the call.

Credit Cards

Some credit cards pay a death benefit at the death of the card holder. Contact the credit card company and ask if that company pays a death benefit at the death of the card holder. Be prepared with the credit card account number when you make the call.

AUTO INSURANCE

If your husband's death was related to an automobile accident contact your auto insurance company and ask what benefits you are entitled to and how to apply.

TO DO LIST

Policies provided by your husband's employer?

❑ Contact employee benefit department.

❑ Ask if husband was covered by a group policy and who is the beneficiary.

❑ If there is coverage and you are the beneficiary, ask the procedure for applying for benefits.

❑ Follow the procedure and apply for the benefits.

Policies purchased by you and or your husband.

❑ Locate the policies.

❑ Contact the insurance company.

❑ Ask who is the beneficiary.

❑ If you are the beneficiary, ask for an application form and instructions for applying for the benefits.

❑ Follow the procedure and apply for the benefits.

❑ If the beneficiary is your minor child, or is deceased, or is your husband's estate, open a probate estate (See chapter 8) and then apply for the benefits.

How do you locate the insurance company?

❑ Contact your insurance agent.

❑ If no agent, call information and ask for a local phone number.

❑ If no local phone number look for the insurance company's address on the policy and write to the company at that address.

❑ Sample letter:

Date
XYZ Insurance Company
123 Boston Boulevard
Detroit, MI 48000

Re Policy 000000

Dear Claims Agent,
    I wish to apply for the life insurance benefits provided by the above referenced policy. Please send me the necessary forms and instructions for applying for the benefits.
    My address is:
    My phone number is:
                                Yours truly,

How do you to apply for benefits?

❑ Complete the claim form the company sent you.

❑ If you have questions that are not answered by the

instructions on the form or in the letter that accompanied the form, call the person whose name appears on the letter.

❏ Write a cover letter:

Date
XYZ Insurance Company
123 Boston Boulevard
Detroit, MI 48000

Re Policy 000000

Dear Claims Agent,
I enclose the completed claim for benefits, a certified death certificate and the insurance policy. Please send the check to me at this address:
Yours truly,

❏ Make a copy of the claim form, the policy and your letter. Mail the original claim form, a certified death certificate and policy to the company.

❏ LASF.

❏ Record on your Reminder Calendar the date the check should arrive.

❏ Fill in the amount of the life insurance proceeds in Section I of the Inventory.

Fraternal Organizations

❏ Is there a policy from a fraternal organization?

❏ If yes, apply for the benefits.

Cancer Policies

❏ Is there a policy that pays a benefit if your husband's death was caused by cancer?

❏ If yes, apply for the benefits.

Credit Union

❏ Do you have a loan from a credit union?

❏ If yes, contact the loan department and ask if the loan includes a death benefit.

❏ Have your loan number and account number ready when you make the call.

Credit Cards

❏ Some credit card companies pay a death benefit at the death of the card holder.

❏ Call the credit card company and ask if your husband's credit card includes a death benefit.

❏ Have the credit card account number ready when you make the call.

Auto Insurance

❑ Contact your auto insurance company if your husband's death involved an automobile.

4

APPLYING FOR SOCIAL SECURITY AND OTHER BENEFITS

Your objective in Chapter 4 is to apply for Social Security and other similar benefits that you may be entitled to.

If you are entitled to Social Security or other similar benefits, you will not receive the money until you file a claim with the appropriate agency. So, the sooner you get the ball rolling by applying for the benefits, the sooner you will receive the money.

SOCIAL SECURITY

Will I receive Social Security benefits?

You are probably entitled to Social Security survivor's benefits if:

- You are 60 or older.

- You are 50 or older and disabled.
- You are caring for a child under 16 or caring for a disabled child who is entitled to benefits.

Will my children receive benefits?

Your children may be entitled to benefits if:

- The child is the child of your deceased husband, and
- The child is:
  1. under 18; or
  2. under 19 and a full-time elementary or secondary student; or
  3. 18 or over and under a disability, and the child was dependent upon your deceased husband, and
- The child is not married.

Will I receive any other benefits from Social Security?

There are two other Social Security benefits that you may be entitled to:

- **Lump Sum Death Payment**

A lump sum death payment is a one time payment of $255 and is paid in addition to monthly survivor's benefits.

Apply for the lump sum payment at the same time you apply for other survivor's benefits from Social Security.

It is important to note that you may be entitled to the lump sum payment even if you are not entitled to survivor's benefits. **But you must apply for the lump sum payment within 2 years of your husband's death.**

- **Black Lung Benefits**

   You may be entitled to black lung benefits if your husband was entitled to black lung benefits. Apply at your local Social Security office **within 6 months of your husband's death**.

How do I apply for Social Security benefits?
   You apply for Social Security benefits in person at your local Social Security office. But, before you go to the Social Security office, call and ask if you can make an appointment and what documents you must bring with you.

   New applicants for Social Security will have their monthly benefit payment deposited directly into their bank account. Consequently when you apply for benefits, you will need the name of your financial institution and your account number as well as the documents that the Social Security office told you to bring with you.

   Take the necessary documents and file the claim(s). Ask a friend to accompany you. The application process is not difficult but discussing your marriage date and your husband's birthdate may be difficult for you.

Insert all documents and correspondence from Social Security into a folder you have labeled "Social Security."

Will I receive Social Security benefits if my husband worked for a railroad?

If your husband worked for a railroad or for certain companies closely connected with the railroad industry, you will probably receive survivor's benefits from the Railroad Retirement Board rather than from the Social Security Administration.

Apply for survivor's benefits at the nearest Railroad Retirement Board office. There are Railroad Retirement Board offices in most major cities. Your telephone directory or your local post office can help you locate the nearest office.

If my husband was a veteran am I entitled to benefits from the Veterans Administration?

If your husband was a veteran locate his military discharge papers and call the nearest Veterans Administration office. Ask if you are entitled to benefits and, if so, the procedure for applying.

TO DO LIST

Social Security Benefits

❑ Call the Social Security office and ask if you are eligible for:

- survivor benefits
- surviving child benefits
- lump sum death payment
- black lung benefits

and if you can make an appointment and what documents you will need to bring with you to file a claim(s).

❑ Go to the nearest Social Security office, taking with you the required documents, the name of your financial institution and account number, and file the claim(s).

❑ LASF.

❑ Record on your Reminder Calendar the date the first check should arrive.

Railroad Retirement Board

❑ If your husband worked for a railroad, contact the nearest Railroad Retirement Board office.

Veteran's Administration

❑ Locate your husband's military discharge papers.

❑ Call the nearest Veteran's Administration office and ask if you are entitled to benefits and the procedure for applying.

5

DETERMINING YOUR ELIGIBILITY FOR BENEFITS FROM YOUR HUSBAND'S PENSION OR RETIREMENT PLAN

Your objective in Chapter 5 is to determine if you are eligible for benefits from your husband's pension or retirement plan, and, if so, to apply for them.

The sooner you determine if you are entitled to benefits and apply for them, the sooner you will receive the money.

How do I determine if I am entitled to benefits from my husband's pension?

Label a folder with the name of your husband's employer. Call the employer and ask for the department that administers retirement benefits. Ask to speak to the person in charge of survivor benefits and write that person's name and phone number on the folder. To the extent possible, speak to that same person each time you call the department.

Explain that your husband was an employee (or retiree) and ask if you are entitled to survivor's benefits and, if so, how to apply for them. Take notes of each conversation and insert the notes in your folder.

What is the next step if my husband's employer says that I am entitled to benefits?

If you determine that you are entitled to benefits, ask what the procedure is for applying for the benefits and follow the procedure.

If you must complete an application ask your contact person to mail the application to you. Note the date you expect to receive the application on your Reminder Calendar. If you have not received it by the day it was promised, call back and ask when you will receive the application. Refer to your notes of prior conversations as necessary.

Do not hesitate to call your husband's employer if you have questions or if you have not received mail by the date promised. Do not worry about "bothering" them as answering your questions and processing your application is their job. Be persistent—your financial well-being is at stake.

If I am entitled to survivor benefits, what type of benefit will I receive if my husband was employed at his death?

If your husband was employed at the time of his death, you may be entitled to a preretirement spousal benefit. If you are entitled to a preretirement spousal benefit:

a. the benefit will be a percentage of the retirement benefit your husband would have received had he lived to retire;
b. the benefit may not be paid to you until the date your husband would have reached retirement age;
c. the benefit will either be a monthly payment for the rest of your life or a one-time lump sum distribution.

Are there rules that I have to follow if I am to receive a lump sum distribution?

If you are to receive a lump sum distribution, depending on your age, you can choose to either roll the lump sum into your IRA (an IRA rollover) or to take the lump sum immediately.

If you elect to roll the lump sum into your IRA, request a "trustee to trustee" transfer which means the trustee of your husband's retirement plan transfers the lump sum directly to the trustee of your IRA. A trustee to trustee transfer avoids your having to pay a 20% withholding tax on the amount of the lump sum distribution.

Do I take the lump sum distribution or do I roll it over into my IRA?

Consult your tax advisor immediately. The decision you make will determine how much tax you pay and when you pay it.

What type of benefit will I receive if my husband was retired at his death?

The type of benefit that you will receive, if any, will be determined by decisions your husband made prior to his retirement. If your husband was receiving a monthly benefit, you may be entitled to a monthly benefit. However, the amount of the monthly benefit that you will receive will probably be less than the amount that your husband had been receiving.

What if my husband's employer says that I am not entitled to benefits?

If your husband's employer tells you that you are not entitled to survivor benefits, and if you believe that information is incorrect, request a Summary Plan Description and a copy of the latest Participant Statement.

Review the Summary Plan Description and Participant Statement. If you still think that you are entitled to benefits, contact your attorney and ask if he or she is experienced in reviewing a Summary Plan Description and what the fee would be. If the attorney is experienced and the fee seems reasonable, schedule an appointment.

If your attorney is not experienced in reviewing a Summary Plan Description or if the fee seems unreasonable, look for another attorney. Your objective is to schedule an appointment with an attorney who is competent to review the plan description and who will do so for a reasonable fee.

TO DO LIST

❑ Contact employer (or former employer if your husband was retired).

❑ Ask to speak to the person in charge of survivor benefits.

❑ Ask if you are entitled to survivor benefits.

❑ If you are told that you are entitled to benefits, ask how you apply, and apply.

❑ Record on your Reminder Calendar the date you expect to receive an application or form from the employer.

❑ If you have a choice between a monthly benefit and a lump sum distribution, consult your tax advisor for guidance before making the selection.

❑ If you receive a lump sum distribution enter it on Section IV of the Inventory.

❑ If you are told you are not entitled to benefits and if you disagree, ask for a copy of the Summary Plan Description and latest Participant Statement.

❑ If you still disagree, contact an attorney experienced in reviewing retirement plan descriptions. Discuss fees before making an appointment.

6

Organizing and Managing your Finances

Your objective in Chapter 6 is to develop and implement a short-term financial plan, a plan that will see you through the first six months after your husband's death.

Why a short-term rather than a long-term plan?

A plan that will see you through the first six months is sufficient unless you are facing a financial crisis. If you are facing a financial crisis (your expenses exceed your income), get help immediately. Consult a trusted, sensible and competent family member or friend. If you are not facing a financial crisis, implement a short-term plan. After six months, however, it is essential that you develop and implement a long-term financial plan.

What is the difference between a short-term and a long-term plan?

Short-Term Plan:

- you determine your financial needs for the first six months,
- you develop a plan to meet those needs, and
- you implement the plan immediately.

Long-Term Plan:

- you project your lifetime financial needs,
- you develop a plan to meet those needs, and
- you implement the plan.

How do I determine my financial needs for the first six months?

To determine your financial needs you must calculate your monthly cash flow. Your monthly cash flow is the amount of your monthly income minus the amount of your monthly expenses.

How do I calculate monthly cash flow?

Turn to the perforated pages and tear out the pages labeled "Cash Flow." (The Cash Flow section below is identical to the Cash Flow section in the perforated pages.)

In the "Income" section list each source of income and the amount of income that source contributes to your total **MONTHLY** income.

If you receive income from a source less often (or

more often) than monthly, convert the income to its monthly equivalent and then enter it in the Inflow section.

For example, if you receive stock dividends of $300 every quarter, multiply $300 × 4 dividends. Your yearly dividend income is $1,200. Now divide the yearly dividend income of $1,200 by 12 months. Your "monthly" dividend income is $100. ($300 × 4 = $1200 ÷ 12 = $100 per month.)

Next, enter the amount of your monthly expenses in the "Expense" section. If you are billed for an expense less often (or more often) than monthly, convert the expense to its monthly equivalent and then enter it in the Expense section.

For example, if you pay a property tax of $3,000 twice a year, multiply $3,000 by 2 payments. Your yearly property tax expense is $6,000. Now divide the yearly tax expense of $6,000 by 12 months. Your "monthly" tax expense is $500. ($3,000 × 2 = $6,000 ÷ 12 = $500 per month.)

Funeral expenses are not included in the cash flow calculations. I assume you paid the funeral expenses shortly after the funeral. If the funeral expense has not been paid, include it as an expense.

CASH FLOW

Income

Sources	Amount Received Each Month
1. Salary	_____
2. Social Security (Chapter 4)	_____
3. Pension Benefits from Husband's Pension (Chapter 5)	_____
4. Annuity Payments	_____
5. Rental Income	_____
6. Interest	_____
7. Dividends	_____
8. Child Support	_____
9. Other	_____
	_____
Total Income	_____

Expenses

Expense	Amount of Monthly Expense
I. Home	
1. Mortgage or Rent	_____
2. Home Equity Loan Payment	_____
3. Property Taxes	_____
4. Insurance	_____
5. Utilities	_____
Heating Fuel	_____
Gas and or Electric	_____
Water and Sewer	_____
Telephone	_____
Cable TV	_____
6. Repairs	_____
Total Home Expenses	_____
II. Living	
1. Food	_____
2. Clothing	_____

3. Transportation

   a. Auto Loan Payment   _____

   b. Auto Insurance   _____

   c. Gas and Oil   _____

   d. Repairs   _____

4. Pet Care   _____

5. Entertainment   _____

Total Living Expenses   _____

III. Medical

1. Health Insurance Premiums   _____

2. Dental Insurance Premiums   _____

3. Medicare Payments   _____

4. Doctor Visits   _____

5. Dentist   _____

6. Eyeglasses   _____

7. Prescriptions   _____

8. Miscellaneous Medical Expenses   _____

Total Medical Expenses   _____

IV. Installment Loans and
Credit Card Payments

    1. Installment Loan Payment   _____

    2. Installment Loan Payment   _____

    3. Credit Card Payment   _____

    4. Credit Card Payment   _____

    5. Credit Card Payment   _____

    6. Credit Card Payment   _____

    7. Miscellaneous Payments   _____

**Total Loan and
Credit Card Payments**   _____

V. Insurance Premiums

    1. Life Insurance Premiums   _____

    2. Disability Insurance Premiums   _____

Total Insurance Premiums   _____

VI. Taxes

    1. Federal Income Tax   _____

    2. State Income Tax   _____

    3. Local Income Tax   _____

Total Taxes   _____

VII. Education

   1. Tuition   _____

   2. Other Related Expenses   _____

   Total Education Expenses   _____

VIII. Other   _____

Totals of Expenses:

I.   Home   _____

II.   Living   _____

III.   Medical   _____

IV.   Installment Loan and Credit Card   _____

V.   Insurance Premiums   _____

VI.   Taxes   _____

VII. Education   _____

VIII. Other   _____

      Total Expenses   _____

Subtract the **Total Expenses** from the **Total Income**. The difference is your monthly **Cash Flow**.

   Total Income   _____

   Minus Total Expenses   _____

   = CASH FLOW   _____

Now that I know my monthly cash flow how do I develop a short-term plan?

There are only two possible short-term financial plans. Choose the plan that fits your situation. If your monthly cash flow is a positive number implement the "Positive Cash Flow Plan." If your monthly cash flow is a negative number, implement the "Negative Cash Flow Plan."

What is the Positive Cash Flow Plan?

If, after considering all of your expenses, your cash flow is a positive number, your short-term financial plan is to maintain the status quo. Be sure, however, that you have included all of your expenses in your calculation of cash flow. The Expenses section contains a list of the most commonly incurred expenses, but if you have expenses that are not included on the list, be sure you enter them in the section labeled "Other" and include them in your calculations.

What is the Negative Net Cash Flow Plan?

If your cash flow is a negative number, your short-term financial plan is to convert your negative cash flow to a positive cash flow. To convert to a positive cash flow **YOU MUST REDUCE YOUR EXPENSES TO AN AMOUNT WHICH IS LESS THAN YOUR INCOME AND SET SOMETHING ASIDE FOR EMERGENCIES.**

Ruthlessly examine your expenses and eliminate

all nonessentials. Simultaneously refrain from all purchases that are not absolutely essential. Treating yourself to something special is understandable but not possible. You must exercise restraint. If you do not reduce your expenses below the level of your income, you will quickly slide into financial crisis.

Summary of the Short Term Financial Plan:
1. Determine your income.
2. Determine your expenses.
3. Reduce your expenses to an amount which is less than your income and leaves something left over for emergencies.
4. Do not deviate from the plan.

**Good financial habits and a positive
credit history:**
It is important that you develop good financial habits and establish a positive credit history in your own name. To help you accomplish both of these objectives, pay all of your bills each month before the due date.

If you were the "bill payer" before your husband's death, continue with the system that you have been using. If you were not the "bill payer," develop and follow a system that encourages you to pay your bills on time.

For example, open your mail daily, review each bill for accuracy. If a bill seems incorrect contact the person or company that sent the bill and ask for clarification. Place the bills in a folder labeled "Bills To Be Paid."

Twice a month pay the bills that have accumulated in the folder. To help develop the habit of paying bills promptly, write "Pay Bills" at two week intervals on your Reminder Calendar.

On the portion of the statement that you keep for your records write the date you paid the bill and the number of the check you used to pay the bill. Insert your portion of the statement in a folder labeled "Bills Paid."

If you do not have a checking account, open one. It is usually too inconvenient and time-consuming to pay bills in person or by money order. Also consider having your mortgage payment and utility payments automatically withdrawn from your checking account.

What is net worth?

Net worth is the amount by which your assets exceed your debts. Calculating your net worth is the first step in long-term financial planning. The information that you have already listed on the Inventory introduced in Chapter 2 will enable you to calculate your net worth.

Why should I calculate my net worth if it is not necessary for short-term planning?

Even though calculating your net worth is not necessary for short-term planning, knowing your net worth will give you a sense of security if your net worth is more than you expected. If, on the other hand, your net worth is less than you expected, the resulting sense of insecurity will push you to develop a long-term plan as soon as possible.

How do I calculate my net worth?

By now you should have all the information you need to complete the Inventory introduced in Chapter 2. Return to the Inventory and check to see that you have listed all of your assets and debts.

Total your assets. Total your debts. Subtract the debts from the assets. The difference is your Net Worth.

When should I begin long-term financial planning?

On your Reminder Calendar enter "Begin Long-Term Financial Planning" on the six month anniversary of your husband's death.

TO DO LIST

❑ Determine your monthly cash flow by completing the Cash Flow section located in the perforated pages.

❑ Develop a plan to achieve a positive monthly cash flow.

❑ Implement the plan.

❑ On your Reminder Calendar enter "Pay Bills" at two week intervals.

❑ Prepare manila folders for "Bills to be Paid" and "Paid Bills."

❑ Pay all bills promptly.

❑ Calculate your Net Worth by completing the Inventory located in the perforated pages.

❑ Enter "Long-Term Financial Planning" on your Reminder Calendar at the date of the six month anniversary of your husband's death.

7

TAXES

You have two objectives in Chapter 7; to determine if you need to consult a tax advisor now, and to locate and organize the information you or your tax advisor will need to prepare your yearly tax returns.

How do I know if I should consult a tax advisor now or if I can wait until it's time to file my yearly tax returns?
You should consult a tax advisor immediately if:

1. Your total assets exceed $600,000, or
2. You are receiving a distribution from your husband's retirement plan, or
3. Your husband was self-employed, or
4. You and your husband paid quarterly tax payments.

If any of the above apply to you consult your tax advisor.

Competent and timely tax advice is important in these circumstances because:

1. It may be possible to decrease or eliminate an

estate tax by filing documents with the local probate court.

2. If an estate tax is due an estate tax return must be filed and the tax must be paid within nine months of your husband's death. The estate tax return is complicated and should be prepared by an accountant. If the estate tax is not paid within nine months you will owe substantial interest and penalties.

3. If you will receive a distribution from your husband's retirement plan you may have a choice between a monthly payment and a lump sum payment. It is important that you discuss these options with your tax advisor before selecting an option because: there may be time limits that you must adhere to; there may be tax advantages or disadvantages depending on which type of payment you choose and you may qualify for income averaging.

4. If your husband was self employed, his business may have immediate tax liabilities that must be met.

5. If you and your husband paid quarterly tax estimates another payment may be due soon and the amount of the payment may change.

What information do I have to locate and organize to prepare my yearly tax returns?
To be prepared to file your yearly tax returns,

label a folder "199_ taxes." Locate your last year's tax returns and insert them in the folder.

As you receive 1099s from your employer and or from financial institutions insert them in the folder. At year end you should have all the information in the folder that you will need to file your tax returns.

As soon as you have all the necessary information either prepare the returns yourself or schedule a meeting with your tax advisor. Don't procrastinate.

TO DO LIST

❑ Consult a tax advisor immediately if:

- Your total assets exceed $600,000, or
- You are receiving a distribution from your husband's retirement plan, or
- Your husband was self-employed, or
- You and your husband paid quarterly tax payments.

❑ Label a folder "199_ taxes."

❑ Locate last year's tax returns and insert them in the folder.

❑ Add 1099s to the folder as you receive them.

❑ Prepare your yearly tax returns as soon as you have all the necessary information. Don't procrastinate.

8

PROBATE

Your objective in Chapter 8 is to determine if a probate of your husband's estate is necessary, and, if so, to begin the process.

WHAT IS "PROBATE" ?

Probate is a court procedure that transfers ownership and title of the assets of a deceased person to his or her heirs. It involves filing the will (if one exists), having the will accepted by the court, evaluating the assets, paying the deceased's debts, and distributing the remaining assets to the persons named in the will.

If there is no will then the assets are distributed according to the laws of the state in which the probate takes place.

How do I determine if I have to probate my husband's estate?

To determine if a probate is necessary you have to know whose name is on the title of all of your husband's assets. You have that information on the Inventory you completed in Chapter 2.

Retrieve the Inventory from its folder. The Inventory should be complete by now; if not, complete it. Review the column entitled "How Asset is Titled." A probate will be necessary if:

1. ANY asset listed on the Inventory is titled in your husband's name only; or
2. The beneficiary of your husband's life insurance policy or annuity is listed as his "Estate"; or
3. The primary beneficiary of your husband's life insurance policy or annuity is deceased and there is no secondary beneficiary named; or
4. Both the primary and secondary beneficiaries of your husband's life insurance policy or annuity are deceased.

It does not matter if your husband left a will, a probate is necessary if any of the above situations exist.

If a probate is necessary, who will receive my husband's assets if he left a will?

If your husband left a will, the assets that were in his name alone will be transferred to the person or persons named in his will. If you are the person named in the will the assets will be transferred to your name.

What if a probate is necessary and I am not named in the will?

In most states, as the surviving spouse, you will receive a portion of your husband's assets even if you are not named in the will. Consult with an experienced probate attorney.

If a probate is necessary, who will receive my husband's assets if he did not leave a will?

If your husband died without leaving a will, the laws of your state will determine who receives his assets. In most states, the surviving spouse receives a portion if not all of the assets. Consult an experienced probate attorney.

Do I need an attorney to probate my husband's estate?

In most states it is possible to probate an estate without an attorney. But if you live in a large metropolitan area with a busy and crowded probate court or if you don't want the frustration and the responsibility of probate, retain an attorney to probate the estate for you. Definitely retain an attorney to probate your husband's estate if his estate is more than $600,000.

If you decide to retain an attorney, retain an experienced probate attorney. Refer to the "Advisors" section in Chapter 2.

Discuss fees and court costs with the attorney at your first meeting. If you are satisfied with the proposed fees request that the attorney prepare a "Fee Agreement" that documents your verbal agreement. You and the attorney should sign two copies of the Fee Agreement with each of you retaining a signed copy.

When should I start the probate?

It takes many months to probate an estate, so, the sooner you start it the sooner it will be completed.

Do not ignore this situation if a probate is necessary. If there are assets in your husband's name alone, you will not be able to transfer them to your name nor will you be able to sell them without a probate. Act now if you have determined that a probate is necessary.

Will there have to be a probate at my death?

If, at your death, there are assets titled in your name only, a probate will be necessary.

In the near future you should consult an estate planning attorney (possibly the same attorney who probated your husband's estate) and develop an estate plan for the transfer of your assets at your death.

Enter "Plan my estate plan" on your Reminder Calendar at the nine month anniversary of your husband's death.

TO DO LIST

❏ Retrieve the Inventory you started in Chapter 2.

❏ Complete the Inventory.

❏ Review the "How Assets Are Titled" section.

❏ Are any assets in your husband's name only?

❏ Review the beneficiaries of all life insurance policies AND annuities and determine if:

- the primary beneficiary is deceased with no secondary beneficiary named.
- the primary and secondary beneficiaries are deceased.
- the primary beneficiary is your husband's estate.

❏ If a probate is necessary, consult an experienced probate attorney.

❏ Discuss fees and costs with the attorney and then commit your agreement to writing in a "Fee Agreement."

❏ On your Reminder Calendar enter "Plan my estate plan" at the nine month anniversary of your husband's death.

9

SPECIAL CIRCUMSTANCES

Did your husband own his business? Does his death give rise to a lawsuit?

Your objective in Chapter 9 is to decide if you face special circumstances and, if so, to decide what to do about them.

There are two special circumstances to consider:

- Did your husband own his business?
- Does your husband's death give rise to a lawsuit?

If my husband owned his business what should I be concerned about?
If your husband owned his business consider the following:

1. The payment of your health insurance premiums.
Are your health insurance premiums paid by your

husband's business? If so, make sure that the next premium payment and future premium payments are paid promptly so that there is no lapse in your health insurance coverage.

2. The payment of quarterly tax payments.

Did your husband pay quarterly tax payments rather than have taxes withheld from his paychecks? If so, make sure that the next quarterly tax payment is paid on time and in the correct amount. You may need to consult your tax advisor.

3. The day-to-day management of the business.

Who is running the business? Is there a manager in place? Do you need to step in and manage the business?

4. The sale of the business.

If your husband was in business without a partner, should you sell the business? Seek the advice of a tax advisor, legal advisor, and a trusted and competent family member or friend. Do not make a hasty decision. If possible, wait at least six months before deciding what to do.

5. The sale of his share of the business if he had a partner or partners.

If your husband was in business with a partner or partners you probably will not have responsibility for day-to-day management. But you will have to decide what to do about his share of the business.

If your husband and his partner(s) have a Buy-Sell Agreement, there will be nothing for you decide as the sale of your husband's interest to his partner(s) will be controlled by the Agreement.

If your husband and his partner(s) did not have a Buy-Sell Agreement, you may choose to sell his interest to his partners. Do not allow yourself to be pushed into a hasty decision. Consult with a tax advisor, legal advisor, and a trusted and competent family member or friend. If possible, wait at least six months before making a decision.

6. His pension plan.

If your husband funded his own pension plan, contact the plan administrator and ask how you file a claim as beneficiary. You will find the name, address and phone number of the plan administrator on the pension plan statements. Consult your accountant before you receive a distribution from the pension plan.

Does your husband's death give rise to a lawsuit?

If your husband's death was accidental, related to his employment, or the result of improper medical treatment there is the **possibility** of a lawsuit. You should consult a personal injury attorney and ask him or her to evaluate whether or not a lawsuit is indicated.

Contact your legal advisor and ask the deadline

(statute of limitations) for filing the appropriate lawsuit and for a referral to a personal injury attorney.

Note on your Reminder Calendar the date which is halfway to the deadline for filing the lawsuit. For example, if the deadline for filing a lawsuit is one year from your husband's death, at the date of the six month anniversary of his death write "Make appointment with personal injury attorney." As painful as it will be to relive the circumstances of his death, don't procrastinate. If the lawsuit is not filed within the appropriate deadline you will lose your opportunity to file a lawsuit.

TO DO LIST

If your husband owned his business:

❑ Does the business pay your health insurance premiums? If so, make sure the premiums are paid on time.

❑ Are quarterly tax payments due? If so, make sure they are paid on time and in the correct amount.

❑ Who is managing the business?

❑ Postpone for 6 to 9 months, if possible, decisions about the sale of the business.

❑ Is there a Buy-Sell Agreement? Seek advice regarding the value of the business before you agree to sell.

❑ Apply for survivor's benefits from your husband's pension plan.

Does your husband's death give rise to a lawsuit?

❑ If appropriate consult a personal injury attorney.

❑ Diary the deadline for filing a lawsuit on your Reminder Calendar.

10

How to Solve Problems Not Discussed in This Book

Your final objective is to determine if you have a legal or financial problem not discussed in this book and, if so, to develop a plan for solving the problem.

You may have a situation or problem not discussed in the preceding chapters. If so, do not ignore it or consider it unimportant just because it's not covered in the book. Instead, apply the same procedure that you have used to resolve your other legal and financial problems:

1. Identify the problem.
2. Consult resources and advisors as necessary.
3. Develop a plan for solving the problem.
4. Implement the plan.
5. Do not procrastinate or delay. Delay may be costly and there is satisfaction and pleasure in exercising control over your life again.

A Final Word Of Encouragement

By reading the chapters and completing the To Do Lists you will regain control of your life and you will begin to feel self- sufficient and secure. Good Luck!

TO DO LIST

❑ Stop and think. Are there any important situations or problems that you have overlooked? If so,

- Identify the problem.
- Consult resources and advisors as necessary.
- Develop a plan for resolving the issue or solving the problem.
- Implement the plan.
- Do not procrastinate or delay.

INDEX

To Do Lists

CHAPTER 1
AS YOU BEGIN

Establish Your Workspace:

"Shopping List":

❑ a box of legal size manila folders

❑ pocket or wall calendar

❑ several legal pads

❑ cheap, easy to use calculator

❑ plain stationery and envelopes

❑ 12" by 18" storage box with cover

❑ roll of stamps

To Do:

❑ Set aside a permanent workspace with desk or table.

" Physical Health"

❑ Eat healthy foods in sensible quantities.

❑ Stock easy to prepare, nourishing and appealing foods.

❑ Meet a friend for lunch or dinner regularly.

❑ Resume former physical activity or,

❑ Buy a pair of comfortable walking shoes, and

❑ Take short walks daily, increasing the distance as you build stamina.

"Emotional Health"

❑ Consider professional counseling.

❑ Ask family or friends for recommendations.

❑ Make an appointment with the counselor.

❑ Locate a support group whose members have lost their spouses.

❑ Learn the date, time and location of the next meeting.

❑ Contact a member and ask them to accompany you to the next meeting.

❑ Go to the meeting.

❑ Seek out other women who have lost their spouses.

❑ Speak to a family member or friend by phone every day.

❑ Make plans for holidays, birthdays and anniversaries.

"Spiritual Self"

❑ Draw from your spiritual resources.

❑ Satisfy your spiritual needs.

A Feeling Of Security

"Shopping List":

❑ extra house keys and an extra car key

❑ magnetic box for car key

❑ timers

To Do:

❑ Give a spare house key to trusted family member or friend.

❑ Conceal a spare house key outside and tell a trusted family member or friend of the location.

❑ Install the timers on TV or radio and conspicuous lights.

❑ Set the timers to turn on the TV or radio and lights when you will be away for an extended period and anytime you come into an empty house after dark.

❑ Conceal a spare car key in a magnetic key box in an accessible place on your car.

CHAPTER 2
GETTING ORGANIZED
TO DO LIST

FROM THIS POINT FORWARD INSTRUCTIONS TO LABEL, ALPHABETIZE AND STORE A FOLDER OR FOLDERS WILL BE ABBREVIATED "LASF"

Identification Numbers

❏ Label a folder

❏ In the folder list husband's:

- social security number
- date of birth
- military service number

❏ List your social security number and your children's numbers if they are minors.

❏ LASF

Documents

Locate:

- ❑ Your husband's will. LASF
- ❑ Tax returns for the last three years. LASF
- ❑ All insurance policies. LASF
- ❑ Your husband's military discharge papers. LASF
- ❑ Fifteen certified copies of your husband's death certificate. LASF
- ❑ Birth certificates for all family members. LASF
- ❑ Your marriage license. LASF
- ❑ Closing or escrow papers received when you purchased real estate. LASF
- ❑ Your divorce judgment if previously divorced. LASF
- ❑ Buy-Sell Agreement and other documents related to your husband's business. LASF

Safe Deposit Box

- ❑ Label a folder "Safe Deposit Box".
- ❑ In the folder list the location and number of the box.
- ❑ Take the key, a note pad, pen or pencil and a briefcase or similar bag that closes securely to the bank and retrieve the box.

❏ Remove these items from the box:

- husband's will
- insurance policies
- military discharge papers
- birth certificates for family members
- marriage license
- real estate documents
- divorce judgment
- documents related to your husband's owner-ship of a business

❏ Make a written inventory of the contents remaining in the box.

❏ Label folders for the items you removed from the box.

❏ LASF.

Advisors

❏ Label a folder "Advisors".

❏ List name, address and phone number of:

- accountant
- attorney
- stockbroker or financial advisor

Reminder Calendar

❑ Record all deadlines on the date of the deadline and a reasonable number of days before the deadline.

❑ Record all items that you are to receive by a certain date on that date.

❑ **REVIEW YOUR REMINDER CALENDAR DAILY.**

Inventory of Assets and Debts

❑ Gather information about each asset and each debt in a separate folder.

❑ Record the value of each asset and the amount of each debt on the perforated Inventory.

❑ LASF for each asset and each debt.

INVENTORY

ASSETS

Type of Asset   **Current Value of Asset**

How Asset is Titled (H = Husband, W = Wife,
J = Joint, T = Asset in a Trust)

Asset	Value	Title
I. Cash Assets		
1. Cash on hand	_____	_____
2. Life Insurance (See Chapter 3)	_____	_____
3. Checking Account(s) (Bank and Credit Union)		
	_____	_____
	_____	_____
	_____	_____
4. Savings Account(s) (Bank and Credit Union)		
	_____	_____
	_____	_____
	_____	_____
5. Money Market Account(s)	_____	_____
	_____	_____
Total Cash Assets	_____	

II. Investment Assets

1. Certificate(s) of Deposit _____ _____

_____ _____

2. Treasury Bills _____ _____

3. Stocks (List the company, number of shares and the current price per share)

Company	Shares	Price Per Share	Total
_____	____	_____	_____
_____	____	_____	_____
_____	____	_____	_____
_____	____	_____	_____

Total Stocks _____

4. Mutual Funds (List the fund, number of shares and the price per share)

Company	Shares	Price Per Share	Total
_____	____	_____	____
_____	____	_____	____
_____	____	_____	____
_____	____	_____	____

Total Mutual Funds _____

5. U.S. Savings Bonds _____

6. Municipal Bonds _____

7. Corporate Bonds _____

   Total Investment Assets _____

III. Real Estate

1. Residence _____

2. Vacation Home _____

3. Vacant Land _____

   Total Real Estate Assets _____

IV. Retirement/Pension/Profit Sharing

1. IRA Accounts (Include lump sum distributions rolled over from your husband's pension plan, Chapter 5) _____

2. Keogh Accounts _____

3. Pension/Profit Sharing Plans (401K, Thrift Savings, Stock Purchase) _____

   Total Retirement/Pension/ Profit Sharing _____

V. Miscellaneous

1. Limited Partnerships   _____

2. Notes, Mortgages or Other Debts
   Owed To You   _____

3. Other   _____

                                                          _____

   Total Miscellaneous Assets   _____

VI. Business Ownership (See Chap.9)   _____

   Totals of Assets:

I.   Cash   _____

II. Investment Assets   _____

III. Real Estate Assets   _____

IV. Retirement Assets   _____

V.   Miscellaneous Assets   _____

VI. Business Ownership Assets   _____

   TOTAL VALUE OF ALL ASSETS   _____

DEBTS (LIABILITIES)

Type of Debt	Outstanding Balance
1. Mortgage (Residence)	_____
2. Mortgage (Vacation Home)	_____
3. Home Equity Loan	_____
4. Auto Loan	_____
5. Auto Loan	_____
6. Credit Card	_____
7. Credit Card	_____
8. Credit Card	_____
9. Life Insurance Loan	_____
10. Other Loan(s)	_____
TOTAL DEBT	_____

Insert the Inventory in a folder labeled "Inventory." You will be adding information to the Inventory as you work through other chapters. After you read Chapter 6, calculate your Net Worth.

NET WORTH:

TOTAL OF ALL ASSETS	_____
MINUS TOTAL DEBT	_____
YOUR NET WORTH IS	_____

CHAPTER 3
APPLYING FOR INSURANCE
BENEFITS TO DO LIST

Policies provided by your husband's employer?

❏ Contact employee benefit department.

❏ Ask if husband was covered by a group policy and who is the beneficiary.

❏ If there is coverage and you are the beneficiary, ask the procedure for applying for benefits.

❏ Follow the procedure and apply for the benefits.

Policies purchased by you and or your husband.

❏ Locate the policies.

❏ Contact the insurance company.

❏ Ask who is the beneficiary.

❏ If you are the beneficiary, ask for an application form and instructions for applying for the benefits.

❏ Follow the procedure and apply for the benefits.

❏ If the beneficiary is your minor child, or is deceased, or is your husband's estate, open a probate estate (See chapter 8) and then apply for the benefits.

How do you locate the insurance company?

❏ Contact your insurance agent.

❏ If no agent, call information and ask for a local phone number.

❏ If no local phone number look for the insurance company's address on the policy and write to the company at that address.

❏ Sample letter:

> Date
> XYZ Insurance Company
> 123 Boston Boulevard
> Detroit, MI 48000
>
> Re Policy 000000
>
> Dear Claims Agent,
>   I wish to apply for the life insurance benefits provided by the above referenced policy. Please send me the necessary forms and instructions for applying for the benefits.
>   My address is:
>   My phone number is:
>
>   Yours truly,

How do you to apply for benefits?

❑ Complete the claim form the company sent you.

❑ If you have questions that are not answered by the instructions on the form or in the letter that accompanied the form, call the person whose name appears on the letter.

❑ Write a cover letter:

Date
XYZ Insurance Company
123 Boston Boulevard
Detroit, MI 48000

Re Policy 000000

Dear Claims Agent,
    I enclose the completed claim for benefits, a certified death certificate and the insurance policy. Please send the check to me at this address:
                        Yours truly,

❑ Make a copy of the claim form, the policy and your letter. Mail the original claim form, a certified death certificate and policy to the company.

❑ LASF.

❑ Record on your Reminder Calendar the date the check should arrive.

❑ Fill in the amount of the life insurance proceeds in Section I of the Inventory.

Fraternal Organizations

❑ Is there a policy from a fraternal organization?

❑ If yes, apply for the benefits.

Cancer Policies

❑ Is there a policy that pays a benefit if your husband's death was caused by cancer?

❑ If yes, apply for the benefits.

Credit Union

❑ Do you have a loan from a credit union?

❑ If yes, contact the loan department and ask if the loan includes a death benefit.

❑ Have your loan number and account number ready when you make the call.

Credit Cards

❑ Some credit card companies pay a death benefit at the death of the card holder.

❑ Call the credit card company and ask if your husband's credit card includes a death benefit.

❑ Have the credit card account number ready when you make the call.

Auto Insurance

❏ Contact your auto insurance company if your husband's death involved an automobile.

CHAPTER 4
APPLYING FOR SOCIAL SECURITY AND OTHER BENEFITS TO DO LIST

Social Security Benefits

❏ Call the Social Security office and ask if you are eligible for:

- survivor benefits
- surviving child benefits
- lump sum death payment
- black lung benefits

and if you can make an appointment and what documents you will need to bring with you to file a claim(s).

❏ Go to the nearest Social Security office, taking with you the required documents, the name of your financial institution and account number, and file the claim(s).

❏ LASF.

❏ Record on your Reminder Calendar the date the first check should arrive.

Railroad Retirement Board

❑ If your husband worked for a railroad, contact the nearest Railroad Retirement Board office.

Veteran's Administration

❑ Locate your husband's military discharge papers.

❑ Call the nearest Veteran's Administration office and ask if you are entitled to benefits and the procedure for applying.

CHAPTER 5
DETERMINING YOUR ELIGIBILITY FOR BENEFITS FROM YOUR HUSBAND'S PENSION OR RETIREMENT PLAN TO DO LIST

❑ Contact employer (or former employer if your husband was retired).

❑ Ask to speak to the person in charge of survivor benefits.

❑ Ask if you are entitled to survivor benefits.

❑ If you are told that you are entitled to benefits, ask how you apply, and apply.

❑ Record on your Reminder Calendar the date you expect to receive an application or form from the employer.

❑ If you have a choice between a monthly benefit and a lump sum distribution, consult your tax advisor for guidance before making the selection.

❑ If you receive a lump sum distribution enter it on Section IV of the Inventory.

❑ If you are told you are not entitled to benefits and if you disagree, ask for a copy of the Summary Plan Description and latest Participant Statement.

❑ If you still disagree, contact an attorney experienced in reviewing retirement plan descriptions. Discuss fees before making an appointment.

CHAPTER 6
ORGANIZING AND MANAGING
YOUR FINANCES TO DO LIST

❑ Determine your monthly cash flow by completing the Cash Flow section located in the perforated pages.

❑ Develop a plan to achieve a positive monthly cash flow.

❑ Implement the plan.

❑ On your Reminder Calendar enter "Pay Bills" at two week intervals.

❑ Prepare manila folders for "Bills to be Paid" and "Paid Bills."

❑ Pay all bills promptly.

❑ Calculate your Net Worth by completing the Inventory located in the perforated pages.

❑ Enter "Long-Term Financial Planning" on your Reminder Calendar at the date of the six month anniversary of your husband's death.

Cash Flow

Income

Sources	Amount Received Each Month
1. Salary	_____
2. Social Security (Chapter 4)	_____
3. Pension Benefits from Husband's Pension (Chapter 5)	_____
4. Annuity Payments	_____
5. Rental Income	_____
6. Interest	_____
7. Dividends	_____
8. Child Support	_____
9. Other	_____
	_____
Total Income	_____

Expenses

Expense	Amount of Monthly Expense
I. Home	
1. Mortgage or Rent	_____
2. Home Equity Loan Payment	_____
3. Property Taxes	_____
4. Insurance	_____
5. Utilities	_____
Heating Fuel	_____
Gas and or Electric	_____
Water and Sewer	_____
Telephone	_____
Cable TV	_____
6. Repairs	_____
Total Home Expenses	_____
II. Living	
1. Food	_____
2. Clothing	_____
3. Transportation	

a. Auto Loan Payment _____

b. Auto Insurance _____

c. Gas and Oil _____

d. Repairs _____

4. Pet Care _____

5. Entertainment _____

Total Living Expenses _____

III. Medical

1. Health Insurance Premiums _____

2. Dental Insurance Premiums _____

3. Medicare Payments _____

4. Doctor Visits _____

5. Dentist _____

6. Eyeglasses _____

7. Prescriptions _____

8. Miscellaneous Medical Expenses _____

Total Medical Expenses _____

IV. Installment Loans and
Credit Card Payments

   1. Installment Loan Payment   _____

   2. Installment Loan Payment   _____

   3. Credit Card Payment   _____

   4. Credit Card Payment   _____

   5. Credit Card Payment   _____

   6. Credit Card Payment   _____

   7. Miscellaneous Payments   _____

**Total Loan and
Credit Card Payments**   _____

V. Insurance Premiums

   1. Life Insurance Premiums   _____

   2. Disability Insurance Premiums   _____

Total Insurance Premiums   _____

VI. Taxes

   1. Federal Income Tax   _____

   2. State Income Tax   _____

   3. Local Income Tax   _____

Total Taxes   _____

VII. Education

   1. Tuition   _____

   2. Other Related Expenses   _____

   Total Education Expenses   _____

VIII. Other   _____

Totals of Expenses:

I.   Home   _____

II.   Living   _____

III.   Medical   _____

IV.   Installment Loan and Credit Card   _____

V.   Insurance Premiums   _____

VI.   Taxes   _____

VII.   Education   _____

VIII.   Other   _____

   Total Expenses   _____

Subtract the **Total Expenses** from the **Total Income**. The difference is your monthly **Cash Flow**.

   Total Income   _____

   Minus Total Expenses   _____

   = CASH FLOW   _____

CHAPTER 7
TAXES
TO DO LIST

❑ Consult a tax advisor immediately if:

  • Your total assets exceed $600,000, or
  • You are receiving a distribution from your husband's retirement plan, or
  • Your husband was self-employed, or
  • You and your husband paid quarterly tax payments.

❑ Label a folder "199_ taxes."

❑ Locate last year's tax returns and insert them in the folder.

❑ Add 1099s to the folder as you receive them.

❑ Prepare your yearly tax returns as soon as you have all the necessary information. Don't procrastinate.

CHAPTER 8
PROBATE TO DO LIST

❑ Retrieve the Inventory you started in Chapter 2.

❑ Complete the Inventory.

❑ Review the "How Assets Are Titled" section.

❑ Are any assets in your husband's name only?

❑ Review the beneficiaries of all life insurance policies AND annuities and determine if:

- the primary beneficiary is deceased with no secondary beneficiary named.
- the primary and secondary beneficiaries are deceased.
- the primary beneficiary is your husband's estate.

❑ If a probate is necessary, consult an experienced probate attorney.

❑ Discuss fees and costs with the attorney and then commit your agreement to writing in a "Fee Agreement."

❑ On your Reminder Calendar enter "Plan my estate plan" at the nine month anniversary of your husband's death.

CHAPTER 9
SPECIAL CIRCUMSTANCES
TO DO LIST

If your husband owned his business:

❑ Does the business pay your health insurance premiums? If so, make sure the premiums are paid on time.

❑ Are quarterly tax payments due? If so make sure they are paid on time and in the correct amount.

❑ Who is managing the business?

❑ Postpone for 6 to 9 months, if possible, decisions about the sale of the business.

❑ Is there a Buy-Sell Agreement? Seek advice regarding the value of the business before you agree to sell.

❑ Apply for survivor's benefits from your husband's pension plan.

Does your husband's death give rise to a lawsuit?

❑ If appropriate consult a personal injury attorney.

❑ Diary the deadline for filing a lawsuit on your Reminder Calendar.

CHAPTER 10
HOW TO SOLVE PROBLEMS NOT
DISCUSSED IN THIS BOOK
TO DO LIST

❑ Stop and think. Are there any important situations or problems that you have overlooked? If so,

- Identify the problem.
- Consult resources and advisors as necessary.
- Develop a plan for resolving the issue or solving the problem.
- Implement the plan.
- Do not procrastinate or delay.